COPING WITH

OPIOID ABUSE

Joe Greek

Rosen
YA
New York

Dedicated to the family of Andrew

Published in 2018 by The Rosen Publishing Group, Inc.
29 East 21st Street, New York, NY 10010

Copyright © 2018 by The Rosen Publishing Group, Inc.

First Edition

Library of Congress Cataloging-in-Publication Data

Names: Greek, Joe, author.
Title: Coping with opioid abuse / Joe Greek.
Description: New York, New York : Rosen Publishing, 2018 | Series: Coping | Audience: Grades 7–12. | Includes bibliographical references and index.
Identifiers: LCCN 2017001527 | ISBN 9781508173946 (library bound book)
Subjects: LCSH: Opioid abuse.
Classification: LCC RC568.O45 G74 2018 | DDC 616.86/32—dc23
LC record available at https://lccn.loc.gov/2017001527

Manufactured in the United States of America

CONTENTS

INTRODUCTION

Legendary singer-songwriter Prince died in April 2016 from an overdose of prescription painkiller fentanyl. In 2014, a sixteen-year-old student from Kirkwood High School in Missouri died after injecting heroin, according to the *St. Louis Post-Dispatch*. Though the two couldn't be more different in age and background, they both shared one thing in common: premature death arising from opioid use.

Opioids are a group of drugs that are often used to treat pain. Heroin, usually taken via injection by syringe, is part of the opioid family, too. Together, the misuse of prescription painkillers and heroin has emerged as a global health problem. The problem has been described as an epidemic that is sweeping through the United States and throughout North America. Though public awareness of the issue has only grown in recent years, the destruction the modern generation of opioid drugs has caused has been ongoing for more than two decades.

Initially, opioid-based prescription pain medications were viewed as a positive, life-altering treatment for patients with chronic pain. Many believed that, properly administered, painkillers would be relatively harmless. However, as time went by, the

Oxycodone is one of the many addictive opioid prescription drugs at the center of a national and global epidemic, one that is only growing.

ugly truth about opioids began to slowly emerge—seemingly, many times over the many decades.

Doctors and researchers had not anticipated the addictive nature of opioids. From rural communities to inner cities, prescription painkillers have become a drug of choice. With it, heroin use has spiked as well and overdoses leading to early deaths have soared.

Opioid abusers come from all backgrounds and age groups. Unfortunately, most opioid abusers don't even realize the danger that they put themselves in as they pop a pill for fun, or to relieve pain. Opioids are one of the most addictive substances available, and the consequences can be devastating to both the body and mind.

Many opioid addicts, including teens, generally begin experimenting with painkillers for fun. Sadly, experimentation can quickly get out of hand. An opioid addiction can develop very quickly, after only a handful of uses. A substance addiction can take over your entire life. All other priorities fade, as one's motivation is directed at getting more of the substance. And when an opioid addict can't afford more of it, or otherwise obtain it, they will be willing to go to great lengths to get high, which may include turning to cheaper alternatives (like heroin) or even committing crimes to obtain the drug or money for it.

Many recovering addicts will struggle their entire lives to avoid relapsing. It can be a daily struggle, but it can also be the difference between a life lived and a life cut short. The good thing to remember, however, is that there is hope. You do not have to let opioids take over your life. As a human being, you have the ability and freedom to choose your path in life. As you'll learn in this book, the path of opioid abuse can quickly lead to a life of imprisonment and pain. On the other hand, you will find that you can also take a stand for your health and start to make the right choices today. Coping with reality as someone who abuses opioids is difficult, but the more you know, the better equipped you are to seek help and to help yourself.

CHAPTER ONE

What Are Opioids?

For centuries people have used opioids to treat pain and ailments. Their recreational use is thousands of years old, too. Unfortunately, substances originally created to help people have become a cause for great concern.

Opioids have come under increasing scrutiny in recent years as the death toll from fatal overdoses of prescription painkillers has soared. Sadly for many people that have found themselves addicted, painkillers are often just the beginning of their journey. Heroin, another form of opioid and one of the most dangerous illegal drugs, has become increasingly popular among teens and adults across the United States.

How Opioids Work

The terms "opioid" and "opiate" are sometimes used interchangeably, but there are differences.

This is a molecular model of codeine, which is an opiate often used as a painkiller, cough suppresant, and anti-diuretic. Its most common use is to relieve mild to moderate pain.

Opiates are derived naturally from the poppy plant, which contains opium. The most common types of opiates are morphine, codeine, and heroin. An opioid, on the other hand, is produced synthetically in a lab. Production of opioids does not require actual opium. Instead, scientists have learned how to create chemical molecules that are very similar to opiates. Some of the most common types of opioids are prescription painkillers, such as methadone, oxycodone, hydrocodone, and fentanyl. On occasion, opioids are lumped in under the larger label of opiates, along with heroin and other drugs.

Though they are manufactured through different processes, opioids and opiates act similarly on the human brain and body. Opioids resemble chemicals that are found naturally in the human body. They attach to tiny nerve cells called opioid receptors. Opioid receptors can be found within the limbic system, brainstem, spinal cord, and throughout other parts of the body.

When an opioid attaches to a receptor, it sends a signal to the brain that produces the "opioid effect." Essentially, the brain releases excessive amounts of dopamine. Dopamine is a neurotransmitter that affects our movement, emotion, cognition, motivation, and feelings of pleasure. The "opioid effect" blocks pain, slows breathing, and creates calm and euphoria.

The human brain and body can become accustomed to receiving the large amounts of dopamine that opioids release. The brain interprets feelings associated with opioids as an award. As a result, overuse can quickly lead to the human brain and body producing a strong desire for the pleasure that the extra dopamine provides.

Scientists have identified three different types of opioid receptors. They are called mu, delta, and kappa. Each receptor provides a different function. The mu receptor, for example, reduces pain and can create pleasurable sensations. Most opioid-based medications have been produced to target the mu receptors. Unfortunately, the mu receptors have been shown to lead to an increase in dependence and abuse, according to the National Center for Biotechnology Information (NCBI). Scientists are continually researching and developing new opioids that don't rely as much on the mu receptors.

Opioids Go Mainstream

How have opioids become so popular and become such a problem? For centuries, humans have used opium from the poppy plant as an analgesic (a painkiller). Laudanum, which is an alcoholic solution that contains morphine, can be traced all the way back to the 1500s. Heroin, one of today's most notorious opioids, was once legal in the United States. To treat menstrual cramps and other types of pain, doctors prescribed heroin up until the 1920s, when Congress banned it.

By the mid-twentieth century, scientists discovered how to create synthetic opiates in the form of opioids. These early forms of opioids, including oxycodone and hydrocodone, were meant for managing

Up until the early 20th century, opium-based medications and other powerful painkillers were sold without a prescription, including ones like the laudanum pictured here.

severe pain and for patients suffering from terminal illnesses. At the time, doctors did not prescribe opioid medications frequently. Even then, it was well known that such analgesics were potentially addictive and led to long-term problems.

However, the reputation of opioids among medical practitioners had improved by the 1990s. One popular physician, Dr. Russell Portenoy, was a vocal supporter of opioid use. Basing his opinions on a study of just thirty-eight patients, Portenoy claimed that opioids were a "gift from nature," according to an article in the Week. He also claimed that less than 1 percent of users experienced addiction. Simultaneously, pharmaceutical companies issued similar verdicts. It wasn't long until millions of Americans were being prescribed painkillers as a solution to ailments such as back pain and osteoarthritis.

Studies and the public record have since disproven that opioids are completely safe. So, why do doctors prescribe such medications if they are so dangerous? Simply put, there have not been many alternatives for pain control that are easily available to people as a quick prescription from a doctor.

A Prescription Gateway

Before the 1990s, when doctors began widely prescribing other kinds of medical opioids to patients,

For centuries, humans have used and abused opium from the poppy plant for pain treatment and recreation. Droplets of the opium secretion, called latex, are shown on this poppy.

heroin was society's main opioid problem. Heroin, which is a natural opiate derived directly from the poppy plant, is often injected from a syringe directly into the bloodstream. Its use is very dangerous for several reasons.

First, most heroin is likely not produced in controlled laboratory settings, like prescription medication. This increases the likelihood that users might introduce other harmful contaminants into their body.

Second, many heroin users share syringes with others, which can easily spread infectious diseases among users. Finally, the government does not regulate heroin and therefore its strength can differ widely among sources. Every addict has a different level of tolerance that they have built up. One stronger-than-normal injection can easily overwork the human body and lead to serious consequences and even overdose and death.

Today, heroin use is experiencing a resurgence across the United States and worldwide. Many observers connect this increase directly to abuse of prescription painkillers. Before today's opioid epidemic, heroin users that could not find the drug would simply be forced to go through withdrawal. Now, it is easier for users to bounce back and forth between heroin and painkillers when one option is not readily available.

Teenagers have become especially vulnerable to the opioid epidemic. Painkillers are often teens' introduction to opioids, and many eventually move on to heroin.

One big reason that heroin in particular has become such a problem today is that it is relatively inexpensive. In many communities, heroin is much cheaper to purchase off the streets than painkillers. While painkillers are very popular, heroin's price can make it extra enticing. Unfortunately, these lower costs make it easier for people to use heroin more heavily and frequently.

Heroin's Appeal Among Youth

A 2015 study from New York University's Langone Medical Center found that three-quarters of US high school students had used opioid-based painkillers before trying heroin. The study of sixty-eight thousand students revealed that more than 12 percent had used potent painkillers such as Vicodin, Percocet, and OxyContin without a prescription. While only 1.2 percent reported using heroin, the survey showed that 77 percent of those had used opioids prior. More alarming, however, is that more than a quarter of the heroin users said they had used the drug more than forty times.

Dr. Joseph Palamar, who headed the study, recommended that drug education programs in schools focus on illustrating the consequences of addiction. His study showed how easily teens can move from opioids directly to heroin. "Teens will be teens, and many teens dabble in a variety of drugs, but narcotic painkillers are one class of drugs they really shouldn't take recreationally," Palamar told *Healthday*. "Dependence can sneak up on you pretty quickly."

For many abusers, heroin addiction is a problem that can follow them for years and even decades. The actor Philip Seymour Hoffman had managed to quit heroin for more than twenty years before a relapse that was been tied to his use of painkillers. In 2014, the *New York Times* reported that Hoffman perished from an overdose of heroin and a combination of other illicit drugs.

The Potential For Misuse

In 2012, the United Nations Office on Drugs and Crime reported that between 26.4 million and 36 million people around the world abuse opioids. The report also indicated that an estimated 2.1 million people in the United States also suffered from substance abuse problems related to prescription opioid pain relievers and approximately 467,000 people were addicted to heroin.

With their great notoriety, why do so many people abuse these substances? Unfortunately, the potential for misuse is very real and difficult to avoid for many people. Individuals that have experienced addiction with other substances are particularly at risk for misusing opioids. In the last two decades, many doctors have prescribed opioids for pain, so young people who are injured in some way, including many athletes, may first get access to them via legitimate means.

Mixing opioids with other substances can be very harmful, too. Alcohol, for example, can intensify certain effects of opioids—their chemical structures are actually similar. Mixing the two can provide an increased sense of euphoria. However, they can also experience a slowdown in their respiratory function. This means that their lungs will not function at the pace the body needs and can result in death by suffocation. Mixing alcohol and opioids can also lead to severe liver problems.

People that suffer from addiction, whether it's related to opioids or another substance, are often unaware or won't accept that they have a problem. For that reason, many addicts will try to reach for increased highs with larger doses. In some cases, even just one more pill than usual is all it takes to induce cardiac arrest or even a coma.

Building Tolerance

Taken properly, opioids are very effective. However, the body's opioid receptors are highly susceptible to developing an increased tolerance to analgesics. Essentially, a person that takes opioids frequently or over an extended period will likely require higher and higher dosages the more he or she uses them.

Another potential side effect of long-term opioid use is called opioid-induced hyperalgesia (OIH). People that develop OIH may experience pains that were not present before taking opioid-based analgesics. With OIH, opioid-based medications can actually lead to sensations of pain rather than pain relief.

As people build up a tolerance to opioids, their risk of dependence increases. The worst outcomes can be both mentally and physically devastating. For individuals that suffer from legitimate pains and ailments, dependence and addiction may go unnoticed because they believe they are treating a problem. People that take opioids for recreation may also believe they have their use under control. Many opioid addicts never see full-blown addiction coming until it's too late.

Researchers continually seek new methods and medications to minimize opioid tolerance. In 2015, as reported by *Forbes*,

The most common paraphernalia used to inject intravenous drugs, such as heroin, are usually unsterile and lead to great risk of infection.

researchers at the National Taiwan University College of Medicine released a study that identified a protein produced by spinal cord tissue as a potential cause behind building opioid tolerance. They found that by blocking the protein—called CXL1—they could minimize the risk of a patient developing increased tolerance to opioids.

A Growing Crisis

The opioid epidemic affecting the United States and spreading internationally has been referred to as the worst drug crisis in American history. Consider that in 1999, motor vehicle deaths outnumbered fatal drug overdoses more than two to one. In 2014, however, fatal drug overdoses outnumbered vehicle deaths by nearly 40 percent, according to PBS's *Frontline*. The shocking

Some dealers traffic in a wide variety of substances. They may entice someone buying gateway substances, like marijuana, into trying harder drugs like opioids.

23

surge in drug-related deaths has caused great concern nationwide—and rightly so, with thirty thousand Americans dying from opioid and heroin overdoses in 2014. According to the Centers for Disease Control and Prevention, in the fifteen-year-period from 1999 to 2014, opioid deaths jumped by 369 percent, while deaths from heroin rocketed upwards by 439 percent.

Two major factors have helped drive this epidemic to where it is now. First, the amount of prescriptions issued by physicians has grown over the years. According to the National Institute on Drug Abuse (NIDA), doctors prescribed seventy-six million opioid prescriptions in 1991. In 2011, the number of prescriptions had almost tripled, to 219 million.

Second, the United States has been flooded with heroin as a result of drug cartel production in Mexico and Latin America. Mexican heroin production alone increased from approximately eight metric tons in 2005 to around fifty metric tons in 2009, according to NIDA. Heroin has become increasingly easier to obtain and cheaper as more product hits the streets.

The opioid and heroin epidemic has impacted nearly every demographic throughout the United States. According to the CDC, whites and Native Americans have seen the largest jump in fatal opioid overdoses. Deaths within these two groups were double and triple the rates of African Americans and Latinos in 2014. The epidemic has not been confined to certain neighborhoods and communities. It has been colorblind to race, gender, and economic status. From rural communities to busy cities, opioid and heroin abuse has taken off.

Myths & FACTS

Myth: If a doctor prescribes it, it must be safe.

Fact: Most medications will be perfectly safe when the patient follows their doctor's directions and strictly adheres to the right dosage. However, many medications can become dangerous with prolonged use, because of the increased risk of addiction.

Myth: If you are able to maintain good grades or hold a steady job, you're not addicted to opioids.

Fact: You may be able to keep your grades up or avoid losing a job, but still have an opioid addiction. Many people believe that they can balance drug use with school or work. However, they often find themselves eventually struggling to stay afloat.

Myth: Addicts can quit whenever they feel like it.

Fact: For most people suffering a form of addiction, quitting is often a long and difficult journey. Opioid addiction, in particular, can be difficult and even downright dangerous because of the potential for severe withdrawal symptoms caused by opioid dependence.

CHAPTER TWO

How Addiction Occurs

Addiction does not happen out of nowhere. It also cannot be attributed to just one factor. In many cases, addiction is the result of a mixture of factors, some controllable, some not. Addiction doesn't discriminate. It can affect anyone, regardless of age, race, or sex. There are many environmental, genetic, and social factors that can contribute to opioid abuse and addiction.

A Product of the Environment

One major factor that increases a person's chances of abusing drugs, such as opioids, is the environment that they are brought up in and live in day to day. One's environment may be defined as one's neighborhood, school, city, and, most important, the home.

The home environment plays a critical role in everyone's development and growth. From

Parents, guardians, and other family members and relatives who engage in addictive behavior can easily have a negative influence on young people, even if their substance of choice is legal.

a very young age, individuals holds older authority figures, especially their parents, in very high regard. Older siblings are also often role models. For better or worse, people tend to emulate parents and siblings and pick up certain habits and traits from them while growing up. Many scientists acknowledge that humans don't actually stop developing mentally until their early twenties.

Sadly, many children grow up in environments where drug addiction, and opioid abuse especially, is their reality. Whether it's a mother or older brother, many children often get their first glimpse of opioid abuse at home. Seeing such behaviors up close, even if a child knows on a gut level that they are bad, can nonetheless help normalize them. A 2013 study funded by NIDA showed that individuals were at a higher risk of drug abuse if their sibling or spouse abused drugs. When it came to siblings, the study also showed that the closer they are in age, the greater the possibility they would abuse drugs.

Most parents and siblings do not want their loved ones to follow in their path and abuse opioids (or any drug), but addiction often overpowers their better judgment. In 2016, for example, an Indiana woman was arrested after being discovered passed out from a heroin overdose in her car, according to Yahoo! News. When police found her, they were shocked to find her ten-month-old baby crying in the backseat.

Heroin and opioid addicts can easily lose consciousness or fall asleep—also known as nodding off—in dangerous situations, such as while operating a motor vehicle.

The mother's addiction had led her to a point in her life where she put her child in danger just to get high.

The Pitfalls of Peer Pressure

Making friends, and trying to fit in, are two of the biggest challenges adolescents are faced with, from junior high school through high school. Research has shown that, like adults, teens will weigh both the risks and rewards they will receive from their actions and behaviors. However, teens often let the potential reward of their actions outweigh other factors. This makes engaging in risky behavior one of the hallmarks of being a teenager.

A 2012 study by NIDA showed that teens were more willing to perform risky driving maneuvers, such as speeding through yellow lights, if peers were watching. Why teens make risky decisions to impress their peers can come down to brain chemistry. The study's researchers monitored the brain activity of teen drivers. The results showed that there was an increase in activity in parts of the brain that are linked to reward. They also deduced that this part of the brain was substantially more active when teen drivers took risks.

As with taking risks while driving and engaging in other activities, teens are also more willing to take risks with drugs such as opioids. Most people understand that opioid abuse is dangerous. However, the reward of being able to fit in with a certain clique or to impress friends can make it easy for teens to disregard the risks that are inherent in opioid abuse. Teens' natural drive to experiment and experience different things also factors in.

Peer pressure is not always about simply fitting in. Another form of peer pressure that most teens will encounter at some point is bullying. According to the National Center for Education Statistics (NCES), nearly one out of every four will report being bullied each year. However, many students will not take the risk of reporting bullying incidents for fear of peer backlash. In environments closed off from adults—like a house party where the parents have gone away for the weekend, for example—someone with a strong personality may easily sway or, in rare cases, even bully others into consuming alcohol or dangerous narcotics.

Fitting in should not require you to take risks that can put your life in danger. Keep an eye out for situations and behaviors that you may be reluctant to engage in, but feel pressure to take part in. Most of the time, your instinct to pass on certain behaviors will be the right one. Of course, it is often hard to pass up acceptance in a group of friends and easier to go with the flow.

Mental Health

Studies have also shown that certain mental illnesses are linked to an increased potential to become addicted to alcohol and drugs. According to a report from the National Bureau of Economic Research (NBER), there is a "definite connection between mental illness and the use of addictive substances." The report found that those diagnosed with some kind of mental health disorder make up a sizeable portion of addicts. This included 69 percent of alcoholics, 84 percent of those who abuse cocaine, and 68 percent of cigarette smokers. Though the report didn't directly study the link to opioids, it notes the very likely connection between mental health and addiction.

One unfortunate pathway for those who suffer mental illness—whether they are prescribed pills to deal with or not—is the tendency to self-medicate. Such individuals don't intentionally set out to become addicts. For example, individuals that suffer from depression may take opioids to help numb the emotional pain they experience. The same can be said for people that suffer from social anxiety. Opioids can help take the edge off stressful situations. However, using powerful narcotics without proper diagnosis and the supervision of mental health or medical professionals is extremely risky.

At first, opioid use may help individuals cope with particular issues—for example, chronic pain from an injury. As time goes by, however, their dependence increases. To obtain the same painkilling result requires higher dosages that also bring higher risks of dangerous side effects.

Another downside to self-medicating is that opioids can potentially have negative interactions with other medications the patient takes. The irony of self-medicating a mental illness with opioids is that it can lead to the rise of other conditions that did no exist before. One of the most perilous is addiction. Addiction is a disease that can affect patients for decades.

Traumatic Triggers

Opioid abuse and addiction can often be triggered by psychological trauma. Psychological trauma can occur when a person has lived in a stressful environment or experienced an event that causes great emotional distress.

Opioids may be prescribed to treat pain from common injuries, but even this can lead unexpectedly to addiction.

Because of age and life experience, a teen's ability to cope with a stressful situation is not often as developed as an adult's. Trauma comes in many forms, including sexual, physical, and emotional abuse. Bullying, for example, can cause students to experience varying degrees of psychological trauma. Common stresses, like accidents that result in injury, can be traumatic, too.

It can be difficult for young children to understand or express their feelings about trauma. As they age, traumas can cause depression and post-traumatic stress disorder (PTSD). PTSD can develop for people who have lived through a terrible event, such as being the victim of rape or a deadly car crash. PTSD is also common among combat veterans.

Taking opioids may give users a feeling of empowerment over situations and feelings they are overwhelmed by. According to the American Psychological Association, approximately 25 percent of children and adolescents will experience a traumatic event before they are sixteen. Psychological trauma can happen to anyone, regardless of age, sex, or race.

When a person is diagnosed with both opioid addiction and psychological trauma, treatment can become more challenging. Nonetheless, there is still hope for individuals that suffer from both. Treatment plans can be tailored to meet the patient's unique needs on both fronts. However, it is important that the person seek help sooner than later.

Friends and the people we choose to associate with can influence our behaviors for better or worse. Still, we may not easily notice that a friend has developed an opioid dependence.

Early Childhood

Researchers have shown that early childhood plays an important role in future behaviors. Certain factors can predispose young people to behaviors such as opioid abuse. For example, a traumatic event during critical stages of development can lead to mental disorders

Positive early childhood experiences can play a vital role in the development of a human being. Many believe that trauma and other problems can predispose us to addictive behavior.

such as depression and social anxiety. If you have suffered from trauma at an early age, and have received counseling and even medication to cope with it, it is important to be on the lookout for telltale signs of addiction in your life. You are among several sub-groups most at risk for falling into addictive behaviors.

The behaviors of parents and siblings, as discussed in a previous section, are also key. What a person perceives as being normal, such as the way one of their siblings acts, helps them determine the way they choose to behave. This can result in good or bad long-term behavior and influence the personality traits someone develops over time. Our early perceptions set us on the path to develop addictive personality traits that may result in opioid abuse as we get older.

Signs of Addiction

Starting out taking opioids recreationally can seem fun at first. They may help with stress or just provide a means of escape. Someone might just do it at parties, for instance. Then it is just at parties and a couple of times a week during the day—maybe after a big exam, or an argument with a friend or family member, to wind down.

You can tell when things are starting to get out of hand, although it tends to creep up on users. There are several symptoms that are telltale signs of opioid abuse. These symptoms may include but are not limited to:

- Drowsiness and frequently falling asleep
- Memory impairment and poor concentration
- Increased anxiety
- Reduced social interaction
- Mood swings
- Slowed breathing and movement
- Apathy and depression

Opioid addiction can cause drastic changes in someone's personality and lifestyle. Someone active in sports or extracurricular activities may become less involved, or even indifferent to their interests, and give them up altogether. Opioid addiction quickly becomes the primary focus in a user's life. He or she may drop off the social map and neglect good friends. New friends might come around, though they may be addicts themselves, or otherwise involved in the drug scene.

From the outside, an opioid abuser may seem less polite, less compassionate, and generally less engaged with people. It's important to remember that addiction is a disease. It can be difficult for addicts to ask for help when they truly need it because their brain convinces them otherwise. Being aware of the symptoms and understanding the powerful nature of addiction is often the first step in helping yourself or someone you know move forward in a positive direction.

Individuals are vulnerable even before they are physically born. Pregnant mothers that smoke or abuse other substances can severely impact the child's future mental and physical development. In fact, babies that are born to heroin addicts often experience painful—and sometimes fatal—withdrawal symptoms. Though we may not be able to recall early childhood, or remember infancy at all, it nonetheless plays a vital role in our future development and ability to cope with the risk factors of addiction.

Our Genetic Makeup

Susceptibility to addictive behaviors can also be traced all the way to the molecular level. Research has shown that our genetic makeup is responsible for more than half of our risk for developing an addiction. Though our genetics are not fully responsible, they can greatly increase our risk of abusing and becoming addicted to opioids.

Our parents and the generations before them pass down our genetic makeup to us. Studies have shown that substance dependence runs in families. Researchers have identified several specific genes that can influence our risk for dependence. However, a particular gene has not been discovered that specifically predisposes someone to addiction.

Interestingly, addiction is genetically inherent in all humans. However, the strength of being predisposed to addiction at the genetic level is not equal in everyone. Some are more prone to addiction than others. Many people, for example, can drink socially without developing an alcohol problem. Others, however, may start out drinking socially but begin to abuse it.

It is important for opioid abusers and addicts to realize that their problem is not necessarily the result of their desire. Our brains are often hardwired to crave certain pleasures that can be associated with opioids and other addictive substances. Every time a person

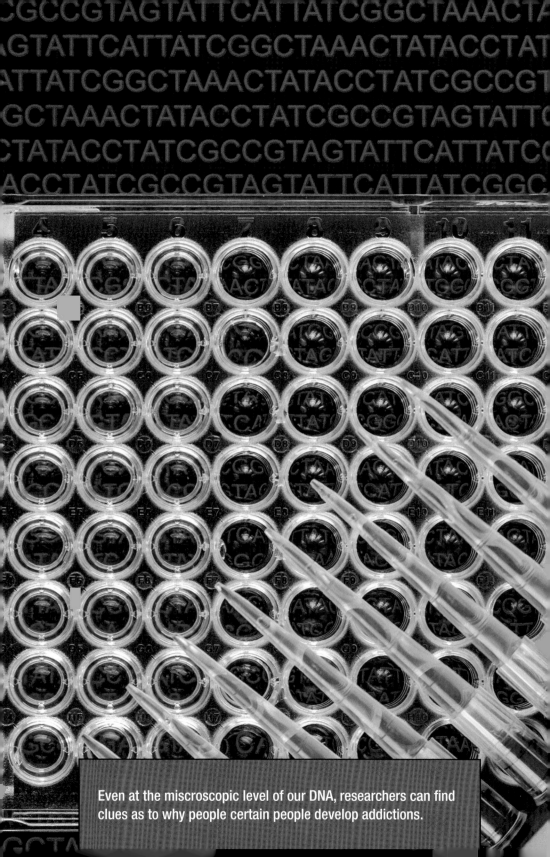

Even at the miscroscopic level of our DNA, researchers can find clues as to why people certain people develop addictions.

abuses opioids, they slightly rewire their brain in ways that leads to dependency. The potential for rewiring the brain to develop an addiction is greater for people that have a history of substance abuse in their family.

Genetic researchers are continually discovering new genes that may influence addictive traits. Their research may one day lead to treatments for patients that can target individual risk genes. New drugs may be able to help rewire the brain of an addict or prevent a potential risk patient from becoming an addict. Though genetics plays a large role in addiction risk, it is not the only determining factor. Addiction is a complex disease that is influenced by several factors. Many people who have a family history of substance abuse are able to lead lives free of addiction.

CHAPTER THREE

Life on Opioids

There are many ways that opioid abuse can impact your life and the life of others around you. Substance abusers, especially as they spiral further down into addiction, lose most perspective or self-awareness of their situation. They cannot really see outside of the problem to judge its negativity or how they are hurting others.

The single-minded pursuit of the drug can destroy all the goodwill and every relationship it touches. Families are torn apart as a result of painkiller and heroin abuse. In this section, we will look at several different ways that opioid abuse can harm you and those that care about you.

How Do Opioids Change Someone?

For many teenagers, academic performance may be the first part of their life that takes a toll from substance abuse. Even if the use begins only occasionally, the more someone is high, the less focus they will have on their studies. Opioids can also impact your memory, which makes it difficult to retain knowledge. Decline in performance at school might contribute to a vicious cycle. The worse someone does, the more disengaged they become, and the more they escape into opioid abuse.

Abusers also may find themselves skipping school and abandoning hobbies and other pleasant activities they used to participate in. Everything that does not revolve around the drug, obtaining it, or procuring money for it, becomes secondary. Eventually, many students that skip school regularly as a result of opioid abuse will end up dropping out altogether.

Alienating Friends and Family

Substance abuse can be a very lonely road to travel. Your peers may feel alienated from you

Substance abusers may not realize that their actions can alienate themselves and the ones they love from each other. Addiction and a tense home environment often go together.

because you have chosen drugs over their friendship. Opioid use encourages the user to disengage socially. Activities like hanging out may no longer bring the same joy that they used to. A general feeling of apathy, or a lack of interest, can easily overtake the abuser's life. For many substance abusers and addicts, the only joy they can find in life is getting high.

For the family of an opioid abuser, the stress of the situation can almost be too much to handle. Tensions at home usually arise when a family member abuses opioids or other drugs. Parents may fight with the child or with each other. Siblings may alienate each other if they perceive the abuser has endangered the family environment.

Additionally, opioid abusers may find they lose the trust their family once had for them. They may not be trusted to watch after a younger sibling or to stay home alone out of fear that they might

When addiction takes hold, finding the next fix will become the individual's primary goal in life. Abusers may even turn to dealing themselves in order to score more easily.

49

steal something of value to purchase more pills. As bad as losing the respect of family and loved ones is, many opioid abusers will lose their self-respect and fall into severe depression. In some cases, the tension and mistrust can lead to an addict leaving home or even being kicked out. Parents may threaten to put their child in rehab or even feel desperate enough to report their activities to the police.

Changes In The Brain

Opioid abuse can essentially hijack the brain. When simple experimentation turns into full-blown addiction, abusers begin to lose control over their life and mind. Addiction will cause a person to continuously crave the sensation that the brain and body experiences from opioids. However, increasing tolerance to opioids will compel the person to seek more. The word "addiction" comes from the Latin term *addictus*, a past tense of *addīcō*, which roughly means "to devote or surrender."

As discussed in other sections of this text, opioid abuse can physically change your brain. Prolonged opioid use can lead to dopamine receptor desensitization. The pathways in your brain will also begin to transform. When this occurs, your thought patterns will begin to take different shapes. The majority of your thoughts and motivations in daily life will be focused on finding opioids. Unfortunately, when addiction gets to that point, your ability to make moral choices becomes compromised.

Researchers also believe that opioids can have negative consequences for your memory and ability to learn new things. For example, some researchers believe that dopamine can interact with the neurotransmitter glutamate and take over the brain's reward-related learning capability. This system helps us by linking essential human activities with pleasure and reward.

Eating is one such reward that can be affected by opioid abuse. Long-term opioid abuse may cause you to no longer gain satisfaction from critical survival needs such as eating. In effect, your mind will no longer see the value in eating as it once did. The power of opioids on the mind should not be underestimated. The brain is very delicate, and some changes are extremely difficult to undo.

Physical Dependency and Withdrawal Symptoms

Developing an addiction to opioids entails your body becoming physically dependent on them. Physical dependence means that your body requires the drug to prevent withdrawal symptoms from occurring. As time passes and use continues without treatment, more of the drug will be required to avoid withdrawal symptoms.

Opioid withdrawal symptoms can include strong mood swings and feelings of depression or despair. Headaches, nausea, and anxiety are also common, and can severely impact one's life.

Each user may develop physical dependency at a different rate. For some, it may take only a short amount of time. Withdrawal symptoms occur when the body does not receive the drug that it has become dependent upon. The withdrawal symptoms that are associated with opioid abuse come in a variety of forms that can affect you physically.

Early symptoms of opioid withdrawal include anxiety, insomnia, sweating, muscle aches, and agitation. Later symptoms may include abdominal cramping, diarrhea, nausea, and vomiting. As you can imagine, the symptoms of withdrawal are not very enjoyable. For some addicts, even beginning to go through them feels bad enough to try to get opioids at any cost.

Depending on the user's dependency level, withdrawal symptoms can range from mild to dangerous. The withdrawal symptoms may start within twelve to thirty hours of the last use of opioids or other addictive substance. It's not uncommon for many opioid abusers to require monitoring while they go through withdrawal. Vomiting and diarrhea can cause dehydration, which can be deadly if untreated.

The process of withdrawal is sometimes called detoxing, or kicking the habit. One of the biggest dangers of going through detox occurs when the user returns to the drug. Detoxing will reduce the opioid abuser's tolerance threshold. Many abusers, however, will use the same dosage that they used before detox. Taking a dosage that was used at the height of a user's dependency may lead to an overdose. Overdoses after detox are a common killer among opioid abusers.

Another Dark Side of Addiction

Opioid abuse and addiction can bring about a host of physical and emotional problems for the user. Another common aspect of opioid abuse that also deserves attention is crime. Drug abuse and crime are heavily linked to one another. Long-term opioid abuse causes changes to the brain that can cause a person to seek and use drugs without regard for the potential consequences.

Because of the financial costs associated with prescription painkillers, many opioid abusers will turn to theft in order to fund their habit. It is difficult to maintain a steady job with a drug habit (though, of course, a small minority manage it occasionally).

It is not uncommon for an opioid abuser to turn to stealing when they are unable to afford their addiction, even if they had never stolen before.

Hence, theft is often viewed as a quick and easy way to achieve the drug user's goals.

Addicts may first turn to easy targets such as family members. Stealing prescribed medication from a parent or loved one may start out with theft of small amounts that may go unnoticed. This may be the way some young people actually become addicted to begin with. Over time, however, the thefts may occur more frequently and involve more pills. Eventually, someone will notice that his or her medications are being taken.

When painkillers are not readily available at home, opioid abusers will turn to outside sources. This may involve breaking into a neighbor's house while they are at work or on vacation. Desperate addicts often steal other valuables that they can then resell in order to purchase from drug dealers. They often turn to burglary, shoplifting, or even armed robbery or worse.

While addiction is considered a disease, the justice system often responds to drug crimes harshly. In many cases, there is little choice. In recent decades, the criminal justice system has seen a surge of drug-related crimes. Many of the crimes are directly involved with opioid abusers that commit theft. Compared to the general population, there are more than four times the amount of criminal offenders with a record that have a substance abuse or dependence problem than nonabusers, according to the National Institutes of Health (NIH).

A Disease to Cure

When you think of the term "disease" you may not immediately make the connection to addiction. However, addiction has been associated with disease for centuries. Dr. Benjamin Rush described alcoholism, another form of addiction, as a disease in the 1700s. The founding of Alcoholics Anonymous (AA) in the 1930s helped increase public awareness and perception of addiction as a disease that required constant and repeated treatment. In the 1950s, Narcotics Anonymous (NA) was established to provide support to individuals that abused substances other than alcohol, including opioids.

There is often debate as to whether or not addiction is actually a disease or a choice. Unlike other diseases, addiction has developed a harsher stigma within our society. This may cause others to overlook the harsh realities that addicts face on a daily basis. Addiction, like any disease, can be difficult to cope with and treat. While everyone may not agree as to whether or not addiction is a disease, the pain it causes the user and his or her loved ones can be just as real as any illness.

The Risk of Overdose

According to the CDC, more than 165,000 Americans died from overdoses caused by prescription opioids like oxycodone and hydrocodone between 1999 and 2014. The growing popularity of heroin use among people aged twelve and older has also been on the rise. Medical treatment for heroin abuse jumped from 277,000 people in 2002 to 526,000 people in 2013. The opioid epidemic will most likely continue to grow for years to come because of the number of prescriptions issued to treat patients and the increasing number of addicts that are turning to heroin as a cheaper alternative. At the same time, the number of overdoses will also continue to grow.

An overdose can occur when a user takes too much of an opioid painkiller. Users may experience depressed or slowed breathing. When this occurs, the body becomes deprived of oxygen. The brain and other internal organs require oxygen to function. Oxygen deprivation can lead to brain damage and even death.

In many cases, a person will not realize they are in danger of an opioid overdose. Mixing painkillers with other substances, such as alcohol, further compromises the health of an opioid abuser. Many overdoses occur during sleep. A person may take painkillers, become drowsy, and fall asleep. Because of the sedative effect on the body's muscular system, the tongue may block the airway during sleep. Asphyxiation, another term for choking, is often the cause of death.

Individuals suffering from an overdose will often appear extremely pale or feel clammy to the touch. Their fingernails and lips may turn purple or blue because of the slowdown of oxygen and blood flow throughout their body. Some individuals will vomit in their sleep and choke to death as a result. Additionally, the heart may slow or stop completely. Overdoses can lead to short-term and long-term comas. Some survivors of overdoses experience varying levels of brain damage because of a lack of oxygen at the time of the overdose.

Children In Harm's Way

One harsh reality of the opioid epidemic is the impact it has on the children of opioid abusers. Young children especially are put at risk when they live in households where opioid abuse is present. Opioid abusers are often too focused on maintaining their habit to pay attention to the needs of their children.

If your parent or guardian is strung out on opioids, daily life at home can range from frustrating, difficult, or simply intolerable. A teenager can fend for themselves, more or less, but even more concerning problems arise if there are younger children around. You may find yourself taking on more responsibilities, adding to the normal workload of your studies, to pick up the slack for the formerly responsible adult or adults in your life. Imagine having to deal with cooking and cleaning to help care for a younger brother or sister, or several siblings, while a parent is emotionally and even physically checked out of reality. Think about the telltale signs discussed so far and whether your parent is exhibiting them.

Depending on how bad things get, you may have to contact relatives, like aunts or uncles, or grandparents, cousins, or whoever else you trust, to intervene in the situation. It may be necessary to get yourself out of the house, and any vulnerable siblings, too. Realize that your parent is sick and needs help and that others may have to take over for the immediate future in caring for your needs and welfare.

The last option, and the one no one should take lightly, is to call someone in authority, like the police or other local or state agency in your area that handles child protective services. Having the police intervene,

Addicts rarely comprehend the actual anguish and stress that they can inflict upon their children or younger siblings. Neglect is often a cruel fact of life for many children of addicts.

or setting the wheels in motion for you or your siblings to end up in foster care or another situation, may be the route to take in a desperate situation.

For example, if there are unsavory, criminal, or violent strangers regularly visiting your home, they may be putting your parent, you, and others in danger. In the worst-case scenario, people may harm your family. An irresponsible addict can be a big danger, even if he or she means no harm. Heroin addicts sometime start fires by nodding off while in the middle of heating up dope for injection or smoking a cigarette. Others might ignore dangerous conditions or situations while high, leaving children or others to suffer for it.

Battling Addiction

If you believe that you or someone you know might have an opioid abuse problem, it is easy to feel discouraged or hopeless. But remember that recognizing the problem is the first positive step in a long journey. Substance abuse and addiction does not have to remain an endless struggle. There are plenty of resources and help available to those that truly want it.

The road may feel dark and the effort pointless at times, but you have to remember that it is a feeling that most reformed substance abusers have felt at one point or another.

Taking A Stand (For Yourself And Your Health)

The most difficult part of dealing with an opioid abuse problem can simply be admitting that you have a problem. Hardcore opioid abusers will by

Realizing you need to treat your addiction can be scary. The road ahead without a substance to fall back on can seem uncertain.

their very nature be hard-pressed to see the gravity of their situation. Opioid abuse can rewire one's thinking process, into believing that a problem does not exist.

Taking a stand against a substance abuse problem can be scary and even downright terrifying. Opioid abusers have to endure their biggest fears: withdrawal and living their life sober. The lingering desire to return to opioids, or otherwise self-medicate, often haunts addicts for a long time. Many if not all addicts consider themselves addicts for life.

First and foremost, your quality of life will never improve as long as you continue to abuse opioids. When most of your friends are going to college and starting careers and families, you could find yourself in the depths of addiction. Substance abuse often leads to isolation from friends and family, which can lead to long bouts of depression. Depression can then reinforce the addiction.

Unstable living situations are common for those addicts who

cannot maintain their addiction and provide for rent and other overhead. Many opioid addicts cycle in and out of homelessness. Those who have ended up stealing or engaging in other crimes often find it very difficult to mend relations with loved ones they have betrayed in some way.

Additionally, long-term opioid abusers are at much greater risk of premature death than the general population, or casual users. Overdoses are extremely common as abusers become more risky in their substance intake. Many heroin users also end up catching dangerous illnesses and diseases from sharing syringes with other users.

Admitting that you have a problem and cannot control it will help you grasp the reality of your situation. It may sound silly, but just saying it aloud in an empty room could even bring some clarity. The realization of your situation will help you break the walls down that hold you back. You will then recognize what a truly awful situation you are in and begin to take steps to correct it.

Removing Yourself From Temptation

One pitfall that can hamper your chances of recovery is your social environment. For teenagers, the group of people that you choose to associate with will be one of the leading factors that leads to long-term recovery or relapse. Choosing to cut off negative influences will make it more likely that you achieve your recovery goals. This is easier if the friends you normally got high with are separate from other longtime friends you may have.

You'll need to ask yourself how you will be able to say no if your primary group of friends are opioid abusers. Is there more to your relationships with these friends than drugs? Substance abusers tend to attract each other because they share one interest: getting high. In the long-term, most addicts are not very dependable friends. It's doubtful you will find much enjoyment together outside of drug abuse.

When and if you decide to cut ties with certain people in your life that could endanger your chances of recovery, you may feel guilty. It's never easy to shake the feeling that you are abandoning or letting someone down. Keep in mind: your choice to break free from a dangerous situation or crowd will enable you to regain your freedom.

At the same time, you may also be the weight that prevents another opioid abuser from freeing himself or herself from addiction. As hard as it may sound, the best way out of a dangerous situation can be to to simply pack up and leave altogether. You have to be able to live your life and love yourself before you can truly be a dependable friend to someone else.

Somone with a problem might care little about what others think about them when they get high. Addicts also have the habit of putting themselves in dangerous and vulnerable positions.

Asking For Help

It is common for opioid abusers or addicts to feel ashamed of their problem and be particularly ashamed to ask someone else for help. For some, asking for any kind of help is considered a sign of weakness. As strong as anyone feels himself or herself to be, no one has super powers. Having the courage to ask for help, and admit one's vulnerability, takes great strength in and of itself.

One big mistake is to insist to yourself that you can handle this problem alone. Unfortunately, the vast majority of opioid abusers have gone too far to be able to quit easily or decisively. Pride is a roadblock that prevents many opioid abusers from being able to move forward. You have to remember that pride will only get you so far and that it will not take care of your physical and emotional health when addiction has control.

You should also not feel embarrassed about asking for help. The thought of telling your parents or a doctor may even cause anxiety.

Still, you need to remember that there are people that truly care about you and only want to help you get on the path to recovery. Overcoming your emotional doubts and fears will help you become stronger as a person even beyond recovery.

Finally, you should not be scared about asking for help. Recovery from an opioid abuse problem will require some of the hardest personal work you've ever done. As time goes by, you will become stronger and find joy in places that you never did before, or perhaps had even forgotten about. Fortunately, no matter where you are in your battle with opioid abuse and addiction, it is never too late to ask for help. You may stumble again and again, but there is always hope.

Offering Help And Staging An Intervention

You may know someone that is addicted to opioids, perhaps a close friend or even a family member. It can be very hard to watch someone that

For addicts, asking for help is one of the most difficult steps forward to take. It both indicates you realize the severity of the problem, but must then follow through on that first step.

you care about struggling. It can also be hard to bring up the tough subject of addiction with them. You may fear driving them away. However, you shouldn't feel powerless to intervene. Rather than withdrawing, your loved one might be ready to take the step to recovery, and you may very well be their chance.

Establishing a line of communication with an addict can prove to be a very delicate situation. Someone confronted about their drug use or resulting behavior may be initially irritated and may even become angry and even verbally combative. In many cases, they will outright deny that a problem exists. However, there are some tips that you should keep in mind if you plan to offer help.

First, avoid blaming the individual for having created the situation that they are in. Even though their actions may have hurt you, other friends, or even other family members, you need to remember the addict's frame of mind. In their more lucid moments, they may be anxious and even fearful. Blaming an addict for the pain they have caused may also increase the guilt that they feel. This may actually increase their desire to get high again. This is because dealing with their emotions, or taking full stock of their behavior, is one main reason people get high in the first place.

Second, don't talk down to the person. You may feel a sense of anger or resentment toward them, but becoming preachy and lecturing them may just fuel

One way to help someone (or yourself) is through group therapy. Talking about one's addiction and the problems that led to it is a common part of many recovery programs.

their own hostilities. Try to remain calm, positive, and nonjudgmental when bringing an abuse problem up.

A Delicate Approach

Finally, don't engage in a conversation with the person when they are high. Someone that is high on an opioid will not have the best control of his or her emotions.

Going Cold Turkey

Addiction to opioids can occur within just a few weeks, or even days (for some), of regular use. Quitting an opioid will likely lead to a number of withdrawal symptoms. Many opioid addicts will attempt to quit by themselves by going cold turkey. The term "cold turkey" means to completely quit a drug without the aid of medication or slowly reducing the amount of drug used over time. Most

Going cold turkey, while admirable, can be extremely tough. Many addicts fail to stay sober. Enlist help from a doctor or someone else if you decide to take this sometimes dangerous route to recovery.

opioid abusers that quit cold turkey will begin with a strong sense of determination. However, once the withdrawal symptoms take effect, the individual will become increasingly likely to relapse.

Going cold turkey, in some cases, can even be deadly. One of the issues with the detoxification process is that a substance abuser's emotions can jump from high to low. Feelings of depression and helplessness are very common among opioid abusers that go cold turkey. For those reasons, the potential to harm one's self or even commit suicide are increased because the pain can feel so unbearable. While going cold turkey may sound like a good idea and even achievable, substance abusers should consult with a physician before taking any drastic steps to quit using.

They may also unfortunately have little recollection later about your conversation, and any promises you extract from them—for instance, to get help or do better—might not mean very much at all, if they plan on honoring them at all to begin with.

Additionally, don't forget that you are not alone either. Reach out to other family members and friends to stage an intervention. An intervention is when a group confronts a substance abuser or addict together.

They share their thoughts on the situation and how they have been personally and negatively impacted by the individual's actions.

This scenario can help show the person that they are not alone and have a support group that is ready to help them seek assistance. As is the case with a one-on-one confrontation, keep the prior points in mind when staging an intervention. The last thing opioid abusers will want to feel is outnumbered and ganged up on by people they perceive as looking down on them.

Getting Treatment

There are several treatment options available for people that have developed opioid dependency and addiction. These include treatments that aim at helping the user understand their addiction and identifying ways to overcome their behavior. Additionally, researchers have developed a variety of medications that can be used to help wean a patient off painkillers and heroin. These drugs may not be the best option for everyone, of course. But they tend to be a good bet for those who have tried and failed before to go cold turkey or to ease off an addiction gradually.

Because of the dangers associated with withdrawal symptoms, medical supervision is sometimes necessary for patients that have developed high dependency needs. In many cases, an addict who requires critical care and observation may be able to take part in a hospital detoxification program.

Another popular option for opioid abusers is joining a residential addiction treatment program. In this case, a patient stays at a facility that specializes in addiction treatment and therapy. These programs can last anywhere from one to six weeks or more. Some of the more intensive programs last three to six months.

The benefit of a residential program is that patients can be placed in facilities that are not located in their community. This helps them avoid dangerous environments and peers that could lead them to a relapse. Many such programs do not allow patients to have access to phones or computers, so that they can focus directly on their recovery.

There are some opioid abusers that don't require the full-scope services of a residential program. In these cases, outpatient treatment programs may be a good fit. An outpatient program is similar to a residential program except that the individual does not have to live at the facility. During an outpatient treatment, the patient participates in therapy sessions as an individual and, in some cases, a group setting.

In addition to behavioral treatment, patients may benefit from the use of medications that are designed to reduce opioid dependency. Medications can be especially helpful during the detoxification stage, when a patient is most likely to relapse. These medications work in a similar way to opioids, by interacting with the body's dopamine receptors. Some medications used to treat addictions, such as Methadone for heroin users, can cause long-term dependency. Some people stay on methadone for a long time. For them, it is a trade-off that is well worth it, if it prevents them from abusing heroin.

Every opioid abuser has unique needs and challenges that only a trained professional can adequately address. Treatment programs can be very helpful in the short-term. However, opioid abuse and addiction generally requires more long-term assistance through therapy and support groups.

10 Great Questions to Ask an Addiction Counselor

1. Can a person get addicted if they take a painkiller only once in a while?

2. If I'm taking a painkiller that was prescribed to me, can I become addicted?

3. What local resources are available to people who are at risk of becoming addicted to opioids?

4. How can I help a friend I suspect is abusing painkillers?

5. Is it dangerous to quit opioids all at once if I have been using them frequently?

6. Can someone become addicted to more than one substance at the same time?

7. How can I avoid being pressured by my peers into taking a painkiller for fun?

8. What advice would you give to someone who has a family member who is abusing opioids?

9. How should I tell my parents that I think I have an opioid abuse problem?

10. Why should I ask for help if I am taking painkillers for fun and don't feel like I have a problem?

CHAPTER FIVE

The Long Road to Recovery

Recovery from opioid abuse is not something that can be easily achieved in a short period of time. Though initial treatments may help and perhaps even yield positive results quickly, you will need to be prepared to face the realities surrounding substance abuse. One of the most important is remaining ever-vigilant in avoiding falling back into old habits, and thereby opening up the door to relapse. Many people consider addiction to be a lifelong condition—one is never quite cured. When you've made the decision to stay sober for life, you may also need outside support. Fortunately, help is available for long-term success, for those who choose to help themselves.

Thinking Long-Term

A short-term recovery program will generally last anywhere from two weeks to an entire month.

A drug counselor will not sugarcoat the harsh truth: many addicts face a long and often tough road out of addiction, and it can appear bleak at times.

Some individuals that are not heavily addicted to opioids may benefit from a short-term program.

For more serious and hardcore cases, however, these programs will not provide enough time for the patient to truly address their issues. To that point, a study by NIDA contends that addicts need to participate in a program that is at least ninety days or longer in order to improve their chances of full recovery. Unfortunately, long-term rehabilitation programs can be very expensive. Additionally, many insurance plans may only provide coverage for a short-term recovery program.

It's important to think long-term if you are challenged by opioid abuse problems. Substance abusers may be able to live a life of recovery for weeks, months, and even years before something triggers a desire to use again. Because many people do not have the luxury of using a long-term rehabilitation program, it often comes down to personal strength and building one's self up again from the ground up.

Take time to identify the triggers in your life that may cause you to want to use. Triggers can come in all sorts of forms, including people and places. You may find that certain environments or relationships cause you unnecessary stress, which leads to a desire to tune out. Even walking or driving by certain places may bring up memories of using. This can easily translate into an itch to use that you find progressively harder to resist.

But remember: it is you who has the power to make changes to your life. Addicts need not repeat the past. Fortunately, there are many supporting resources that can help addicts understand their addiction and specific, potential triggers.

Support Groups

Opioid and substance abusers may often feel isolated from people or from the world around them. The problem they face, however, is not an isolated one. Remember, there are millions of people that are in the same shoes as you are. Many of them are young. The value of joining a peer support group can be invaluable to their long-term recovery. They key is to stay strong, and avoid becoming an older person telling a group of younger people about their years-long struggle of kicking and going back to heroin, for example.

Support groups are safe places to receive nonjudgmental support and discuss the challenges that face all opioid abusers. Being a part of a group helps addicts minimize the feelings of isolation and shame that lead to using again. Members help each other remain positive and motivated to achieve long-term sobriety.

Narcotics Anonymous (NA) is perhaps one of the most popular groups that supports recovering addicts. NA support groups are widespread and more likely than not available in your community. Whereas Alcoholics Anonymous (AA) is targeted to alcoholics specifically, NA is open to individuals with any variety of substance abuse problems. You may also find a nearby support group through local nonprofit organizations, churches, and government-assisted programs.

One decision a recovering addict must make is whether to use prescription medications in a long-term effort to quit. If so, they must also figure out how much, and when to wean themselves off.

One of the key aspects of many support groups is the use of a sponsor. Sponsors are former addicts that provide support to individuals that are trying to remain sober. Your sponsor will become a vital part of your long-term recovery as they coach you through strong urges that are common during recovery. Once you have reached a milestone in recovery and have stayed sober for a certain amount of time, you may feel the call to become a sponsor and pay it forward.

Avoiding the Old Crowd

Friendships and romantic relationships can be some of the most rewarding parts of your life. Part of what makes you who you are is the group of people that you choose to surround yourself with. However, the people you believe to be your closest allies can also turn out to be the biggest triggers for choosing opioid abuse over sobriety.

Narcotics Anonymous and the Twelve-Step Program

Narcotics Anonymous began in Los Angeles in 1953 as a peer support program to help substance abusers and addicts. Since then, the program has expanded to provide services across the world. One of the primary foundations of NA is the twelve-step recovery program. This method uses twelve points that focus on the need for social support and the belief in a higher power, which is not specifically associated with any particular religion. The twelve steps are as follows:

1. We admitted that we were powerless over our addiction; that our lives had become unmanageable.

2. We came to believe that a Power greater than ourselves could restore us to sanity.

3. We made a decision to turn our will and our lives over to the care of God as we understood Him.

4. We made a searching and fearless moral inventory of ourselves.

5. We admitted to God, to ourselves, and to another human being the exact nature of our wrongs.

6. We were entirely ready to have God remove all these defects of character.

7. We humbly asked Him to remove our shortcomings.

8. We made a list of all persons we had harmed, and became willing to make amends to them all.

9. We made direct amends to such people wherever possible, except when to do so would injure them or others.

10. We continued to take personal inventory and when we were wrong promptly admitted it.

11. We sought through prayer and meditation to improve our conscious contact with God as we understood Him, praying only for knowledge of His will for us and the power to carry that out.

12. Having had a spiritual awakening as the result of these steps, we tried to carry this message to addicts, and to practice these principles in all our affairs.

Substance abusers and recovering addicts may have a difficult time recognizing the damage that has been done to their life as a result of toxic relationships. It can be even more confusing, because most friends seem (and usually are) sincere in their friendship. Nonetheless, opioids and other addictive substances can easily cloud one's better judgment.

Just because friends care about each other doesn't necessarily mean that remaining friends is possible in the short term or long term, if opioids figure in. Opioids and other drugs tend to destroy friendships by playing people against each other. Given a choice between loyalty to a friend and loyalty to the drug, most addicts pick the latter. If you've made the important decision to take control of your future and avoid opioid abuse, you will have to make difficult decisions about whom you associate with.

As you move forward, take stock of those that you choose to be around. Ask yourself if certain individuals pose a risk to your sobriety and long-term wellbeing. You may even come to realize that your shared interests don't really go much farther than opioids.

After you have built up enough confidence and strength, and are confident in your recovery, you can even offer help to old friends who are struggling with opioid abuse or addiction. However, you have to keep in mind that a person will have to make an effort on his or her part to change lifestyles. Make sure that if you open your heart and door to friends to talk things over—such as lending them a helping hand in helping them kick a habit—they respect your sobriety. This means they should not show up to a meeting with you high or otherwise intoxicated.

Addressing Concurrent Disorders

The issue of recovering from addiction and substance abuse problems can be complicated by concurrent disorders. A concurrent disorder can be any variety of mental or physical health issues or other addictions that an individual has in addition to a substance abuse problem. For example, a person that has developed an opioid addiction may have already had social anxiety.

In many cases, a concurrent substance abuse or other health issue may be directly related to one another. Mental health issues can easily trigger a desire to take opioids in order to tune out the underlying problem. By treating just one issue, however, the individual may quickly relapse. For that reason, it's important to work closely with certified professionals to identify concurrent disorders in order to find proper treatments.

The majority of people who suffer from concurrent mental health and substance abuse problems need to

For addicts with concurrent disorders, going it alone is usually not the best option. Rather, they should consider counseling, drugs, and other treatmens to treat two or more problems simultaneously.

plan their treatment approaches carefully. A family doctor may be able to provide treatment to individuals who have mild to moderate disorders. Those who suffer from severe disorders, however, often require specialized care.

Treatments for concurrent disorders and opioid abuse problems may involve medications and therapy. Support groups, for example, may become part of the advised treatment. Additionally, there are numerous types of psychotherapeutic treatments, including cognitive behavioral therapy (CBT). CBT is a short-term therapy where patients are taught how to understand how their thought patterns shape the way they see the world and themselves. Therapy can play a critical role in helping substance abusers understand the underlying reasons for their actions. Without truly grasping why we are the way we are, it can be difficult to make the right decisions into the future.

Alternative Treatments for Chronic Pain

Chronic pain often leads people to develop opioid abuse problems. Unfortunately, many people have been prescribed opioids as a quick and easy treatment for pain. Suffering from chronic pain can be devastating. On the other hand, adding an opioid addiction to the equation can make things even worse.

According to the CDC, "opioids are not the first-line therapy for treatment of chronic pain outside of active cancer treatment, palliative care, and end-of-life care." In fact, there are a variety of treatments available that individuals with chronic pain may benefit from. Over-the-counter acetaminophen, which is an active ingredient in Tylenol, is a common pain reliever that is not addictive. Nonsteroidal anti-inflammatory drugs (NSAIDs) are another form of medication that can also help address chronic pain. Certain forms of antidepressants can also help reduce pain by treating nerve, muscular, and skeletal pain.

Physical therapy is another alternative form of treatment for chronic pain. This involves certain exercises that can help build strength and relieve pain long-term. Generally, a certified physical therapist will be needed to identify specific exercises that will be helpful. Additionally, doctors recommend exercise to the majority of patients. Yoga and jogging,

Exercise and physical fitness, such as yoga, can help recovering addicts maintain their health and also give them something to focus on, rather than dwelling on a return to a toxic lifestyle.

for example, can help improve your blood circulation and lead to better overall health. The added benefit of exercise is that it can be an addictive experience that is beneficial to your health.

Other alternative treatments for chronic pain include massage, acupuncture, and chiropractic care. If you suffer from chronic pain and are looking to stay away from opioids or to get off of them, be sure to consult with your physician first. Your doctor may know of great alternative treatments that would help your specific ailment.

The Future Is Yours

If you've overcome an opioid abuse problem or are looking to begin the path to recovery, just keep in mind that your life is what you make of it. With all the information outlined in this book, you may be closer to understanding the true gravity of the problem that exists. However, books and words of advice from loved ones and educated researchers will not solve the problem.

The burden of opioid abuse will always fall on the back of the abuser. For many, it will be a life-long struggle that will require strength and resolution to persevere. You may fall down as you walk the path of sobriety. In fact, you may fall down several times. Still, take solace in knowing that you can always get

The future may seem uncertain, both when beginning recovery and at many points along the way. However, the important thing to remember is to take thngs one day at a time, and to not lose hope.

back up. Better yet, you can always build yourself up stronger than you were yesterday.

Take this time to reflect on where you've been and what your experience has been like. Ask yourself if a life of substance abuse is the way you want to spend your time on this planet. There's a world of opportunity available at your fingertips. However, the opportunities and dreams you have will never be had without a fight.

Opioid abuse has one destination: addiction. Addiction, whether you're there now or later, will consume your existence. It's up to you to intervene and refuse to lose control of your life, because when you do lose control to addiction, it will be very difficult to gain it back. Don't squander your chance to live life to it's fullest. The lives of many people will just become a statistic in research and government reports. Are you more than just a number?

Glossary

addiction A condition where someone feels a strong sense of desire or need for a substance, thing, or activity.

anxiety A sense of worry or unease about something.

chronic Describes a pain or condition that persists for a long time, sometimes even permanently.

coma A state of unconsciousness that can last for an indefinite period of time and can be caused by injury or illness or induced by medication or by drug overdose.

depression Feelings of deep sadness or low spirits, now recognized as a real disorder by mental health professionals.

detox The process of quitting a substance and the period of time it takes for the substance to leave the body.

epidemic To occur on a widespread scale and often relating to health.

milestone A significant action or event that marks the beginning or end of one stage of human development.

neurotransmitter A chemical substance found in the human body that transmits signals from one nerve fiber to another.

overdose An excessive dose of a drug that can be dangerous or deadly.

painkiller A medication that is used to relieve or neutralize pain.

peer A person of the same age, social group, or rank or class as another.

premature To occur before a scheduled or expected time.

rehabilitation To restore something to its original state of being.

relapse When someone that has abstained from substance abuse begins to use again.

synthetic A substance created through artificial means, which imitates or is very similar to one that occurs in nature.

terminal illness A disease with no existing cure or treatment that is expected to lead to death sooner rather than later.

tolerance The amount or dosage of a substance that a person's body can handle before succumbing to illness or death.

trauma An intensely disturbing experience that can cause emotional distress that lasts temporarily or long term.

withdrawal A reaction, or set of reactions, within the body that occurs when someone stops taking an addictive substance.

Betty Ford Center

Hazelden/Betty Ford

39000 Bob Hope Drive

P.O. Box 1560

Rancho Mirage, CA 92270

(866) 831-5700

Website: http://www.hazeldenbettyford.org/treatment/locations/betty-ford-center-rancho-mirage

The Betty Ford Center is a drug recovery facitlity, and has a long history of treating substance abuse since its founding in 1982.

Canadian Centre on Substance Abuse (CCSA)

75 Albert Street, Suite 500

Ottawa, ON K1P 5E7

Canada

(613) 235-4048

Website: http://www.ccsa.ca

The Canadian Centre on Substance Abuse raises public awareness to reduce the harm of substance abuse on society. Through research, the organization nurtures the exchange of knowledge to help guide policy making to improve the health and safety of Canadians.

Drug Free Kids Canada (DFK Canada)

PO Box 23013

Toronto, ON M5N 3A8

Canada

(416) 479-6972

Website: http://www.drugfreekidscanada.org

Drug Free Kids Canada is a nonprofit organization that strives to prevent the abuse of painkillers and illegal substances by teenagers. The organization promotes awareness and education and offers advice on treatment for substance abusers in Canada.

Nar-Anon Family Groups

23110 Crenshaw Boulevard, Suite A

Torrance, CA 90505

(800) 477-6291

Website: http://www.nar-anon.org

Nar-Anon Family Groups is a peer support group that provides counseling and group therapy to friends and families of addicts. Similar to Narcotics Anonymous, the group also uses a twelve-step recovery program to help overcome the situation of living with or knowing a substance abuser.

Narcotics Anonymous (NA)

PO Box 9999

Van Nuys, CA 91409

(818) 773-9999

Website: https://www.na.org

Narcotics Anonymous is a nonprofit organization dedicated to providing resources and help to individuals with substance abuse problems. The organization offers peer support groups, peer-to-peer counseling, and other helpful resources for overcoming addiction.

National Institute on Drug Abuse (NIDA)

6001 Executive Boulevard

Room 5213, MSC 9561

Bethesda, MD 20892-9561

(301) 443-1124

Website: https://www.drugabuse.gov

The National Institute on Drug Abuse is a government-funded organization that functions to advance science and research on the causes and consequences of drug use. NIDA promotes awareness of substance abuse and addiction as well as treatments that can benefit public health.

SMART Recovery

7304 Mentor Avenue, Suite F

Mentor, OH 44060

(866) 951-5357

Website: http://www.smartrecovery.org

SMART Recovery is a regionally-based recovery
support group. The organization is dedicated to
helping individuals overcome addiction through
self-empowerment and self-directed change.

Websites

Because of the changing nature of internet links,
Rosen Publishing has developed an online list of
websites related to the subject of this book. This site
is updated regularly. Please use this link to access
the list:

http://www.rosenlinks.com/COP/opioids

Adams, Taite. *Opiate Addiction—The Painkiller Addiction Epidemic, Heroin Addiction and the Way Out.* Washington, DC: Rapid Response Press, 2013.

Bestor, Sheri Mabry. *Substance Abuse: The Ultimate Teen Guide* (It Happened to Me). Lanham, MD: Scarecrow Press, 2013.

Brezina, Corona. *Heroin: The Deadly Addiction* (Drug Abuse and Society). New York, NY: Rosen Publishing, 2009.

Carlson, Hannah. *Addiction: The Brain Disease.* Branford, CT: Bick Publishing, 2010.

Higgins, Melissa. *Living with Substance Addiction* (Living with Health Challenges). Edina, MN: Essential Library/ABDO, 2012.

Kenney, Karen. *The Hidden Story of Drugs* (Undercover Story). New York, NY: Rosen Publishing, 2014.

Lew, Kristi. *The Truth About Oxycodone and Other Narcotics* (Drugs & Consequences). New York, NY: Rosen Publishing, 2014.

Lyon, Joshua. *Pill Head: The Secret Life of a Painkiller Addict.* New York, NY: Hyperion, 2010.

Marshall, Shelly. *Young Sober and Free: Experience, Strength, and Hope for Young Adults* (Second Edition). Center City, MN: Hazelden Publishing, 2016.

Parks, Peggy. *The Dangers of Painkillers* (Drug Dangers). San Diego, CA: Referencepoint Press, 2016.

Sheff, David. *Clean: Overcoming Addiction and Ending America's Greatest Tragedy*. Boston, MA: Houghton Mifflin Harcourt, 2014.

Williams, Rebecca E., and Julie S. Kraft. *The Mindfulness Workbook for Addiction: A Guide for Coping with the Grief, Stress and Anger that Trigger Addictive Behaviors*. Oakland, CA: New Harbinger Publications, 2012.

Wolny, Philip. *The Truth About Heroin* (Drugs & Consequences). New York, NY: Rosen Publishing, 2014.

Amico, Chris, and Dan Nolan. "How Bad is the Opioid Epidemic." *PBS Frontline*, February 23, 2016. http://www.pbs.org/wgbh/frontline/article/how-bad-is-the-opioid-epidemic.

Arlotta, CJ. "Study Proposes New Therapy To Suppress Opioid Tolerance." *Forbes*, February 19, 2015. http://www.forbes.com/sites/cjarlotta/2015/02/19/potential-new-therapy-to-suppress-opioid-tolerance/#27b056be5cfb.

Bellum, Sara. "Why Does Peer Pressure Influence Teens To Try Drugs." DrugAbuse.gov, May 8, 2012. https://teens.drugabuse.gov/blog/post/why-does-peer-pressure-influence-teens-try-drugs.

Bellum, Sara. "Your Environment May Influence Drug Use." DrugAbuse.gov. October 17, 2013. https://teens.drugabuse.gov/blog/post/your-environment-may-influence-drug-use.

Bock, Jessica. "Heroin's Youngest Addicts Are Dying in High School." *St. Louis Post-Dispatch*, February 8, 2016. http://www.stltoday.com/news/local/metro/heroin-s-youngest-addicts-are-dying-in-high-school/article_60be2c42-d87c-5f1a-915a-0b5d6b56abd4.html.

Carey, Benedict. "Prescription Painkillers Seen as a Gateway to Heroin." *New York Times*, February 10, 2014. http://www.nytimes.com/2014/02/11/

health/prescription-painkillers-seen-as-a-gateway-to-heroin.html?_r=0.

Durieux, Marcel, and Christina J. Hayhurst. "Differential Opioid Tolerance and Opioid-induced Hyperalgesia: A Clinical Reality." *Journal of the American Society of Anesthesiologists*, February 2016. http://anesthesiology.pubs.asahq.org/article.aspx?articleid=2474170.

Inside Edition staff. "Mom Pictured Holding Syringe While Allegedly Overdosing With Infant Son in Car: Cops." Yahoo! News, October 26, 2016. https://www.yahoo.com/news/mom-pictured-holding-syringe-while-212300193.html.

National Alliance of Advocates for Buprenorphine Treatment staff. "How do opioids work in the brain?" NAABT.org, December 2008. https://www.naabt.org/faq_answers.cfm?ID=6.

Reinberg, Steven. "Painkillers Often Gateway to Heroin for U.S. Teens: Survey." *HealthDay*, December 29, 2015. https://consumer.healthday.com/kids-health-information-23/adolescents-and-teen-health-news-719/painkillers-often-gateway-to-heroin-for-u-s-teens-706080.html.

Smith, David. "The Evolution of Addiction Medicine as a Medical Speciality." *American Medical Association Journal of Ethics*, December 2011. http://journalofethics.ama-assn.org/2011/12/mhst1-1112.html.

Thaler, Malcolm. "Why Is Opioid Addiction Happening to So Many of Us?" LiveStrong.com, August 29, 2016. http://www.livestrong.com/article/1012275-opioid-addiction-happening-many-us/.

Week staff. "America's Painkiller Epidemic, Explained." Week, February 13, 2016. http://theweek.com/articles/605224/americas-painkiller-epidemic-explained.

Vanderah, TW. "Delta and Kappa Opioid Receptors as Suitable Drug Targets for Pain." National Center for Biotechnology Information, January 26, 2010. https://www.ncbi.nlm.nih.gov/pubmed/20026960.

Volkow, Nora. "America's Addiction to Opioids: Heroin and Prescription Drug DrugAbuse.org, May 14, 2014. https://www.drugabuse.gov/about-nida/legislative-activities/testimony-to-congress/2016/americas-addiction-to-opioids-heroin-prescription-drug-abuse.

Index